Kabbalah

MADE EASY

Kabbalah
MADE EASY

Maggy Whitehouse

BOOKS

Winchester, UK
Washington, USA

First published by O-Books, 2011
O-Books is an imprint of John Hunt Publishing Ltd., Laurel House, Station Approach,
Alresford, Hants, SO24 9JH, UK
office1@o-books.net
www.o-books.com

For distributor details and how to order please visit the 'Ordering' section on our website.

Text copyright: Maggy Whitehouse 2010

ISBN: 978 1 84694 544 1

A CIP catalogue record for this book is available from the British Library.

Design: Lee Nash

Cover image by Jon Cooper Taylor

Illustrations by Peter Dickinson

Printed in the UK by CPI Antony Rowe
Printed in the USA by Offset Paperback Mfrs, Inc

We operate a distinctive and ethical publishing philosophy in all
areas of our business, from our global network of authors to
production and worldwide distribution.

CONTENTS

Acknowledgments

To the work and inspiration of Z'ev ben Shimon Halevi without which I would never have continued to study, let alone under- stand, Kabbalah.

To the members of Halevi's London study groups, 1993-2009 — too many to mention by name — whose insights, journeys and teaching have formed an integral part of my work.

To the members of my husband's and my own Kabbalah study groups who have inspired me to learn more and more.

Introduction

When I first started studying Kabbalah my mother was so concerned that she went to ask her vicar what he thought. After consulting a dictionary, he told her that it looked like I had become involved in devil-worship and witchcraft.

This vicar — a lovely man who had sat with me at the deathbed of my first husband — reflected so many people's views of this ancient Judaic tradition of spiritual knowledge. Over centuries Kabbalah has often been misused, debased and misrepresented and it has been used for strange and sometimes unsavory magical practices. But it is a tool, like electricity: it can be used for whatever purpose you wish and it needs to be used with care. It is intended to guide and instruct the spiritual seeker and for me it was the roadmap that I needed to make peace with a Christianity that had condemned my young husband to hell because he was an atheist.

Kabbalah is regarded as primarily Jewish and it has been kept safe within the Jewish nation for centuries. There is still some opposition to the idea of non-Jews and women studying it but, again, it is a tool. It is not a religion and it either fits into the hand of the seeker or it does not.

In 2007 I finally made peace with the religion of my birth and was ordained into an independent sacramental church by a bishop who is both a mystic and a Kabbalist. But it was the Jewish guiding light within Kabbalah that piloted me through years of seeking, falling and crying out in the wilderness until I found my own path to understanding both the Holy One and myself. And if I had to, even now, choose just one faith to which I would subscribe, it would be Judaic mysticism. Jesus was a Jewish mystic and what's good enough for him is good enough for me.

Could I have learnt my Kabbalistic knowledge from just one book like this one? Absolutely not. But this kind of book might have helped in the years when I was tangled up in finding out what Kabbalah actually was; when being both a woman and non-Jewish meant I was sometimes perceived as an outsider, an intruder; a loose cannon and even a threat. It would have been good to have had a simple beginner's guide that said "Listen, it's just one system. Yes it works, yes you can study it whatever your faith. But it's not a required system of learning. It is just one valid and useful form of showing you that you are a reflection of God."

All of Kabbalah is summed up in the translation of the Great and Holy Name of God: "I will be that which I will be" (Exodus 3:14). God and the Universe will reflect back to me that which I reflect back to them.

Kabbalah is a structure. *We* are the form that this structure will take in the 21st century. We are the coat of many colors, the "coat of skin" that will interpret Kabbalah for future generations. With the Grace of the Holy One, we will do a good job and help others to find their own, individual, paths to the Source of All. And hopefully, in doing so, we will honor the Judaic tradition that has kept Kabbalah safe for so many centuries so that we may comprehend its gifts now.

1

What is Kabbalah?

Kabbalah is a Hebrew word meaning "receive." If you walk into a hotel in Israel you might well see the word "Kabbalah" directing you to the reception area. This is a lovely irony because many people over centuries have tried to make Kabbalah complex, secret and forbidden when it was originally intended to be a roadmap showing us our path in life.

This ancient mystical tradition is based on a structure called The Tree of Life. Most people equate Kabbalah with Judaism but this diagram is a matrix that can help us to understand the relationship between God, the Universe and humanity whatever our religion or system of belief.

The only thing required to study Kabbalah is a belief in a Higher Power.

Kabbalah is called the Western mystery tradition because it is the esoteric teaching behind the three Abrahamic religions of Judaism, Christianity and Islam. Much Kabbalistic Teaching can be found in both the Old and New Testaments of the Bible and in the Talmud, the Jewish commentary on Torah. Once understood, Kabbalah can be used to make these apparently obscure teachings much clearer.

However, Kabbalah is not a religion; it is a tool to help us in our path of self-realisation and spiritual development whether we choose to use the Bible or not.

Kabbalistic spiritual practices worldwide include:

- Contemplating and chanting the names of God in Hebrew.

- Painting the Tree of Life as a mandala.

- Contemplative meditation to encounter and heal aspects of our inner psyches.

- Theurgy (sacred magic) of the Angels.

- Astrology.

- Understanding the levels of ego, self, soul and spirit.

- Studying Biblical texts for patterns that relate to the Tree of Life.

- Interpreting life and history through the Tree of Life, observing both our own patterns and humanity's development.

- Discussion, leading to greater understanding and spiritual growth.

2

Red String Theory

One of the things most commonly associated with Kabbalah is a red woolen string worn on the wrist in order to avert the evil eye. This is not strictly Kabbalistic; rather a form of folk-lore that extends throughout the Eastern world. The red wool bracelet is particularly associated with the Kabbalah Center but is often confused with the Buddhist red string which is blessed by a lama or teacher and given to a student or visitor to a shrine. The Dalai Lama also blesses red string and ribbon to give to his audiences and followers.

The red wool bracelet is said to be sacred to Kabbalists when it has been wrapped seven times around the tomb of Rachel, one of the Biblical Matriarchs. However, Rachel dabbled in magic and died in childbirth so many modern students of Kabbalah take the view that this is superstition or a magical amulet rather than a sacred practice.

This is a good example of how the tradition updates itself. While "red string theory" is popular it has no connection to The Tree of Life nor with ancient written teachings. The expensive purchase of the Kabbalistic woolen thread takes into account how hard it is to get genuine articles that have been taken, by Jews, into the occupied territory where Rachel's tomb stands. However, the Buddhist strings are blessed by a living teacher and given free.

3

The Numbers Game

Kabbalists often work with the patterns of numbers.

- Ten refers to the ten circles or *Sefirot* of the Tree of Life which represent ten different aspects of God, of us and the Ten Commandments.

- Four represents the four levels of being. The Tree is repeated at four levels for the four primary elements of earth, water, air and fire. Ten times four represents a whole cycle of life — a length of time for completing a project or the passing of a generation (think 40 years in the desert or 40 days in the wilderness). Four also represents the four suits of the Tarot.

- Twelve is also sacred, representing the ten Sefirot together with the non-Sefira of Da'at — of which more later — and the observer (you). Twelve is also the twelve tribes of Israel and the twelve signs of the zodiac.

- Three refers to the three top Sefirot, known as the Supernal Triad and representing the first attributes of God. From this we get the first idea of Trinity and the concept of One God with masculine and feminine aspects.

- Seven refers to the seven lower Sefirot but also to the concept of four plus three (four worlds or levels, three aspects of the Divine). There are seven churches, seven seals, seven spirits, seven trumpets etc. in the Book of Revelation.

- Twenty two refers to the number of letters in the Hebrew alphabet, the number of paths between the Sefirot on the Tree of Life and the 22 cards of the Major Arcana in Tarot.

Used sparingly, the numbers game can be very useful. The Biblical Book of Esther, for example, has ten chapters and describes the growth of the lead character's soul according to the attributes of the ten Sefirot. However, focusing on the numbers can go on and on and get very complicated. In fact, many would-be Kabbalists get lost in the symbolism of numbers and forget that the system is meant to be for developing the soul rather than advanced mathematics.

There is also *Gematria* a mathematical system which assigns a numerical value to each of the 22 letters of the Jewish alphabet and looks for matching words or phrases in the Bible in order to seek out patterns and meanings with the same numerical value. One of the best-known versions of Gematria is the numerical value placed on the names of God. Ironically for a tradition rooted in Judaism, which was the first great monotheistic religion, this system gives God dozens of different names in addition to the ten Sefirot aspects of Divinity.

The best-known of these is the 72 names of God which is actually a 72-syllable name from a sequence of letters in the Book of Exodus. This in turn is part of a 216-letter name of God. If you really want to spend your whole life in the world of Gematria you can also work with a 304,805-letter name of God revealed by reciting all the letters of the Torah in a particular sequence.

N.B. *Bible Codes* or *Torah Codes* interpret the Bible through the number of spaces between letters rather than by the numerical value of the letters themselves. This too is a way of tying yourself up in knots if you aren't careful.

Nowadays, many Kabbalists focus more on contemplation of the Hebrew letters that make up the variety of names for aspects of God. It is believed that it is not necessary to understand the

Hebrew letters or words in order to be able to use them as a powerful tool for meditation.

4

The Oral Teaching

Kabbalah is an oral teaching passed on by word of mouth and updated for each generation. How it stops becoming Chinese Whispers in the process is because of its unique, basic structure of The Tree of Life (fig 1, overleaf) which uses a matrix of Divine and human attributes known as *Sefirot* (Hebrew for "circle").

The Tree of Life is like the skeleton of a mammal. The bones are all in the same order for every beast but the posture and the outer design of each beast is unique even if the differences are very subtle. So whatever the outer appearance, a Kabbalist can always check back to the structure of the teaching. It's more of a language that resides in the heart than an external system.

This book is about the 21st century interpretation of that basic, timeless structure. It will be appropriate for 20, maybe 30 years but the next generation will always have new insights to share.

The diagram of the Tree represents a perfect human being — the image of God. But it is also the image of the blueprint of every individual human being. For each of us, the goal is to be balanced in the centre *Sefira* which is called Tiferet. Then we are centered; in touch with our active and receptive sides (the right and left columns) and connected with the Source (above) and in charge of our ego and body below.

Tiferet is Hebrew for both "truth" and "beauty." The two names work wonderfully together because bare truth can be harsh and ugly and beauty on its own can be dishonest. But great truth always contains beauty even if it is a fierce, divine beauty.

As well as being an image of the perfect human being, the Tree of Life is a design of how the Universe works which can be just as useful to the orthodox religious believer as to the Biblical

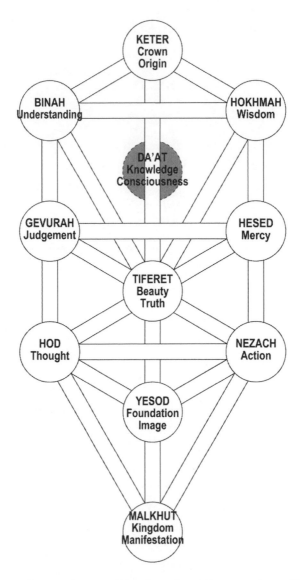

scholar or the modern spiritual seeker. You can be a Kabbalist and a Jew, a Christian, a Muslim, a Pagan, a Hindu or whatever faith you like.

Just as the spaces between the notes in music are what gives the melody, Kabbalah is the spaces between the words in both Old and New Testaments of the Bible so it is a wonderful tool for bridging the gap between conventional, New Age and spiritual beliefs.

Since the invention of the printing press, Kabbalistic teaching has become more and more complicated and often crystallized in old teachings that may be out of date. However it is meant to be a simple system based on the observation of the patterns within the Universe — the design principles of how everything works — and no matter how many books are written about Kabbalah, it is still a teaching best understood through question and answer. It thrives in groups where discussion is encouraged.

For thousands of years Kabbalah was primarily Jewish. Judaism was the first faith to believe in just one God and the Jewish nation kept the sacred teaching of Kabbalah close to its heart and its mystics used it as a structure on which to base its religion.

Kabbalah "went public" with the advent of the printing press but that was just at a time when it had been completely revised because of the persecution of the Jews in the Inquisition. What emerged – and was first printed — was a 16th century version of the original teaching which was taken up and used by Christian, Alchemical and magical groups.

5

Lurianic Kabbalah

This version, known as "Lurianic Kabbalah" after its mystical founder Isaac Luria, is incredibly complicated, so much so that many people interested in Kabbalah find it too difficult to understand and are put off the whole subject. Ironically, Isaac Luria himself forbade his followers to write down his teachings. However, people are people and his students disobeyed.

As this is *Kabbalah Made Easy* and Lurianic Kabbalah is so difficult, this book will focus on the simplest version of Kabbalah; the closest we have to the original teaching.

There is a second reason for not using Luria's system in this book. All Kabbalah up until his day believed that the world was created perfect (as it says in the Bible "And God saw every thing that He had made and, behold, it was very good" Genesis 1:32). Evil was caused by misuse of human free will. An earthquake or natural disaster was not seen as evil but as a misfortune. How humans responded to it was the only criteria used to define "good" and "evil." It was also believed that our choices determined the quality of our lives.

Luria's Kabbalah came about after the 15th century Inquisition where thousands of Jews who had survived the horror of the *autos de fé* had been expelled from Spain and Portugal. They could not understand how such a terrible thing had happened to them and how a benign God could have permitted so much suffering for his chosen people.

Luria's inspiration was to reveal that when God created the Universe, a mistake was made which led to the Sefirot or vessels which were transmitting the Light of Creation shattering. The shards from these broken vessels (known as *Klippot)* became a form of external evil which attacked the good. This answered the perennial question of "why do bad things happen to good people?" This is very similar to the Christian concept of the Devil which had become stronger in the Middle Ages so Christian mystics found it easy to be in tune with the new, Lurianic, system.

Before this revelation, Kabbalah had believed that creation had been perfect and it was misuse of human free will which was the source of any evil. And, with the modern interest in the Law of Attraction, the concept of personal responsibility and realisation of the effect of our emotions on our lives, has re-emerged simultaneously with the older teaching of Kabbalah.

In the 21st century the best-known version of the ancient teaching is called the Toledano Tradition after the Golden Age of Spain in the Middle Ages. This was when philosophers and sages from Judaism, Islam and Christianity worked together in cities such as Toledo, Granada, Malaga and Cordova.

Neither system is right or wrong; it is simply a matter of personal preference and perception. Both suggest that personal and spiritual development are the way forward for all of humanity with the Lurianic system focusing on our healing the external evils within the world and the Toledano system focusing on healing our own inner imbalance so that we can act skillfully in the world.

This book does not in any way infer that the Jewish nation created or deserved the hideous crimes perpetrated against them in the Inquisition. However it recognizes that once difficult situations arise, they will grow and grow when fueled by negative emotion — unless good people take action for change.

6

The Origin of the Tree of Life

The Tree of Life diagram is based on the seven branched cande-labrum known as the Menorah from the Biblical Book of Exodus (fig 2, opposite). The menorah was made out of one piece of gold smelted from the treasures the Israelites brought with them from Egypt. It was built to a design precisely described in Exodus and placed in the tabernacle of the moveable temple built by Moses and the Israelites in the wilderness. It has been referred to by mystics through the centuries as the source of the oral Torah (Law); the first five books of the Bible and its design and markings represent the Sefirot, the paths and the four different worlds or levels in Kabbalistic teaching.

The first written correspondences between the Menorah and the Tree of Life were outlined by the early Christian Church Father Iraneus, and later by the 18th century mystic Rabbi Moshe Chaim Luzzato. The concept was further developed by the 20th/21st century father of Toledano Kabbalah, Z'ev ben Shimon Halevi.

The Tree of Life design as we know it today is believed to have been adapted from the design of the Menorah by Rabbi Yizhak Saggi Nehor (1160-1235) who was known as Isaac the Blind. The Rabbi or his students are also credited with clarifying Kabbalistic teaching on reincarnation and Karma and naming the Sefirot.

Rabbi Isaac believed that contemplating the aspects of the Sefirot with sacred intention, known as *Kavana,* could bring people into direct contact with divinity.

The Tree of Life has three vertical columns (fig 3, overleaf) and three horizontal ones. The vertical ones represent the following:

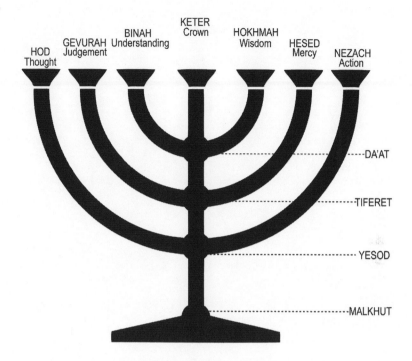

Left Hand Column

- The passive, feminine principle,
- Negative energy
- Contraction
- Receiving

Right Hand Column

- The active, masculine principle,
- Positive energy,
- Expansion
- Giving

Central Column

- Consciousness

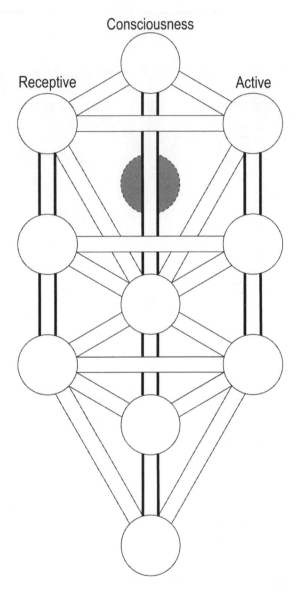

In the modern world, women often take issue with the idea of femininity being associated with negative energy (darkness as opposed to light) and passivity. However all of humanity is a balance between masculine and feminine energy. A human born as a genetic woman can be 51% feminine and 49% masculine and a genetic man 51% masculine and 49% feminine. It follows that we are a blend of both pillars and it is interesting to note that many modern women are prone to over-giving (over-balancing on the right-hand pillar) while wishing that others would give to them.

The central column is where we would stand when in total balance and the middle Sefira, Tiferet, is where we are *all* truly centered with access to all our inner and outer attributes above, below and on each side.

The horizontal columns divide the Tree into four levels representing (from top to bottom):

- Fire, divinity, light and the colour white.
- Air, spirit, thought and the colour blue.
- Water, soul, emotions and the colour purple.
- Earth, body, automatic systems and the colour red.

Kabbalah also has a second diagram, known as *Jacob's Ladder* which expands this principle of four levels or four worlds. The Ladder is four separate Trees each melding with each other and it is used to demonstrate the different levels of Universal principles as well as human ones. For example, the Ladder contains angels at the soul level but archangels at the spiritual level. It got its name from the vision of Jacob in the Book of Genesis. He saw a ladder extending through the heavens down to Earth with angels ascending and descending on it. For more on the ladder see page....

It is worth mentioning in passing that the First Temple of the Israelites was quite different from the Second Temple, the ruins of which still stand in Jerusalem, Israel (the Western Wall). The Second Temple was built in the time of King Ezra and the difference between the two temples and how they were managed was very similar to the changes seen in the Protestant Reformation in Europe. Ezra and his priests saw the old Temple as housing idols and being over-complicated and corrupt. It is believed that the first temple had a Holy of Holies dedicated to the One God and two pillars either side representing the masculine aspect of the Divine (Yahweh) and feminine (Asherah). The four worlds, as represented by the four Trees of Life in Jacob's Ladder were each represented by a great archangelic being: we know them nowadays as Michael (fire), Raphael (air), Gabriel (water) and Uriel (earth) although they had other names at first. People were able to go to the Temple for prophesy, as to the Delphic Oracle in Greece. All of this was forbidden in the Second Temple.

Many early Christians saw Jesus as a force for taking them back to the beliefs and times of the First Temple. The second coming of Christ is shown in the Book of Revelation as being symbolic of a return to First Temple times with the Harlot (the Second Temple) being replaced by the Queen of Heaven (the First Temple).

Both Temples had a veil to separate the Holy of Holies from the rest of the Sanctuary area and this was woven in the four colors of the four worlds: red, purple, blue and white.

7

Different Kinds of Kabbalah

In the modern world, Kabbalah is associated with

- Orthodox Judaism which focuses deeply on the spiritual symbolism and revelation within the sacred letters of the Hebrew alphabet and limits Kabbalistic learning to men aged over 40 who have studied Hebrew and are married. This ruling was brought in after "the false Messiah" Shabbetai Zvi who brought Kabbalah into disrepute in the 17th century.

- The Kabbalah Center which teaches a sometimes controversial New Age version of the tradition and has its own brand including Kabbalah Water, red string and accessories. This is also known as "the Kabbalah of the Famous" because of its popularity with celebrities such as Madonna, Demi Moore and Rosanne Barr. Although it ostensibly follows the Lurianic system, the Kabbalah Centre also teaches the precept of self-responsibility and that our lives are created by our own thoughts and feelings.

- Christian Kabbalah. This came into being after the invention of the printing press made Kabbalistic documents available to all. It thrived during the later Renaissance through Christian scholars who perceived that mystical aspects of Judaism and Neo-Platonism were compatible with Christian thought. It has not become of mainstream interest in Christianity because it became mixed in with occultism in the 18th century.

- Alchemical Kabbalah. Alchemy dates back to pre-Biblical times and has always been closely associated with Hermeticism ("as above so below"). Alchemists are renowned for the search for the Philosopher's Stone and the secret of turning base metal to gold. Kabbalistic Alchemists regard both as metaphors for transforming the base elements of the psyche into the gold of spiritual enlightenment.

- Golden Dawn Kabbalah or The Hermetic Order of the Golden Dawn, a complicated mix of initiation, ritual magic, Rosicrucianism, Egyptology, metaphysics, astrology and Tarot founded by S. L. "MacGregor" Mathers and William Wynn Westcott in the 19th century. It was made famous by the teachings of Dion Fortune and Israel Regardie and infamous by the frightening antics of Aleister Crowley.

- Toledano Kabbalah which takes the teaching back to its pre-Lurianic origins and which, despite its ancient lineage, is the system most in line with modern-day understanding of Karma and the Law of Attraction. This school, led by Z'ev ben Shimon Halevi, is primarily Jewish although it involves those of other faiths as well.

Also worth mentioning as they involve aspects of Kabbalah are:

- Tarot which has a 22-card Major Arcana which is parallel to the 22 paths of the Tree of Life and four suits which equate to the four worlds of the second Kabbalistic diagram *Jacob's Ladder*.

- Freemasonry which shares many Kabbalistic principles and temple-building symbolism from the Old Testament. The temple and the ability of the high priest to pronounce the name of God correctly while in the Holy of Holies was a vital part of the Jewish High Holy days of worship in ancient times. The activities of the high priest within the Sanctuary are featured in the Royal Arch Degree.

- Magic which uses many similar symbols. Magic has come to mean many things in the modern world but in Kabbalah is defined as using personal will to affect the workings of the universe as opposed to aligning ourselves to God's will. An example would be casting a spell to make a particular person love you — which is a violation of the other's free will and carries nasty karmic repercussions.

Kabbalah can be spelt many ways as Qabalah, Qabbala, Cabala or Kabala. There is no "correct" English translation of the Hebrew spelling of: הלבק — Qof-Beit-Lamed or KBL. In Biblical times vowels were never written in Hebrew. This made the language far more flexible than today with many different inter-pretations, nuances and tones available than our translations of the Old Testament would imply.

Different spellings have come down to us today dependent on whether Kabbalah was being taught by Jews, Christians, alchemists or magicians.

Generally the spelling is as follows:

- **Kabbalah:** Jewish mysticism
- **Cabala:** Christian mysticism
- **Qabalah** (and other spellings beginning with a Q): Hermetic, Magical, Alchemical, Occult, Pagan.

A spelling beginning *Qua* is sometimes used but in the English language this is, strangely enough, inaccurate. *Qua* is pronounced as *kwa* as opposed to of *ka* which is the original Hebrew pronunciation. However, the spelling with *Qua* does work in other European languages.

Like many other mystical traditions, Kabbalah has often been abused and, because it was hidden, thought secretive or evil by those who didn't understand it. The English word "cabal" which comes from the same Hebrew root is often used to refer to secretive groups.

This book uses the "original" Jewish spelling of Kabbalah in tune with its emphasis on the oldest, simplest tradition.

8

Kabbalah and the Bible

Legend tells us that Kabbalah (then just known as the Knowledge) was first taught to Adam and Eve as they left the Garden of Eden. It was all contained in what has come to be known as *The Book of Raziel* but, as neither Adam nor Eve could read or write, this refers to an oral teaching or inspiration revealed by the Archangel Raziel, whose name means "Secrets of God."

It was said to be a guide to all celestial and earthly knowledge which would help humanity perfect itself and return to paradise.

It is likely that Kabbalah began as a way of explaining the origin of creation to a people without scientific knowledge. Certainly, it was based on observation of the patterns of the planetary movements in the sky and of the primary elements of fire, air, water and earth as well as direct inspiration.

The Big Bang theory of the Universe exploding out of nothing is an exact reflection of the Kabbalistic teaching that God had to create a space of no-thing-ness in Its Absolute Self in order to start the process of creation. This withdrawal to create a space is known as *zim-zum*. The teaching says that light was poured into the space, or Cosmic Womb, in a pattern of expansion and contraction creating the original matrix of the Tree of Life. There had to be duality in order for the light to be contained, otherwise it would have flowed forever with no form.

The reason behind creation is explained as "God wishing to behold God" or, in more modern parlance, God wishing to give birth to a baby; a reflection of Itself with free will which could experience existence physically, emotionally and spiritually rather than just conceptually. The Tree of Life represents an image of the "divine baby" which is known as *Adam Kadmon*, the primordial human being. It is said that each human being is one cell in the body of Adam Kadmon and each of us is journeying to perfection. When we all have become all that we desire to be then the divine baby will be born and the purpose of creation will be completed. What would happen then is beyond the realms of understanding.

Adam Kadmon has long been referred to by mystics as "the only-begotten" son of God. Christians later gave this title to Jesus of Nazareth who represented the perfect human being on earth. The difference is that Kabbalah teaches that we all can (and eventually will) reach the same level of consciousness as Jesus whereas conventional Christianity teaches that Jesus is the only Christ.

The first human to become perfected, according to the mystical teaching, was Enoch, who is referred to, briefly, in the Book of Genesis and who now is half-human, half-angel as *Metatron*, in the highest heaven.

Kabbalistic teaching was expanded throughout the teachings of the Old Testament, for example, the stories of the Patriarchs and Matriarchs, heroes and heroines each depict a Sefira on the Tree of Life. It was known to many of the great Jewish rabbis including Rabbi Hillel and Gamaliel, the latter reputedly the teacher of St. Paul.

9

Kabbalah in History

As Kabbalah is an oral tradition and one which has often been kept hidden from public view, it is a complex matter tracing its history but several renowned Kabbalists are known to have taught and developed the system. One of the best-known is Solomon Ibn Gabirol an author and mystic who lived in the 11th century.

In the Middle Ages and beyond many books were written about Kabbalah; most of them short examinations of some aspect of the Tree of Life. Ibn Gabirol wrote poetry as well as books, including his famous *Keter-Malkhut* which descended through the Sefirot expressing the majesty of God and the struggles of humanity in mastering our baser instincts. The poem is 40 stanzas long – 4x10 being the number of Sefirot in the four Trees of Life that make up Jacob's Ladder, the Kabbalistic diagram of the Universe. The confessional part of the poem is still used as a prayer on the Jewish Day of Atonement.

Other influential books included *Tomer Devorah*, (The Palm Tree of Deborah) by Moses Cordovero in the 16th century and *Sefer Yezirah* (The Book of Formation) which probably dates from the 10th century but could be up to 2000 years old. The authorship is uncertain and the book itself is mostly about the numerology of the Hebrew alphabet.

In medieval times Jewish men who studied Gematria would seek for patterns in the Torah (the first five books of the Bible). As there are 22 pathways on the Tree of Life, each number held a particular significance based on the attributes of a combination of the Sefirot of the Tree to which the corresponding path was linked.

Probably the most famous book about Kabbalah which is still in use today is *The Zohar* which means "Book of Splendor." As with the *Sefer Yezirah* there is great dispute about the origin of this book: some people date it back to the 2nd century CE and others to the Middle Ages. It was first published in 13th century Spain by a Jewish writer called Moses de Leon who claimed to have found dozens of ancient texts written by a second century Rabbi called Simeon ben Yohai in a cave in Israel. The book does refer to historical incidents which happened after the 2nd century but some say that these are Nostradamus-like predictions.

The Zohar is a mystical interpretation of the Talmud, which, in turn, is a commentary on the first five books of the Bible. There is an old saying about the Jewish nation "two Jews, three opinions" which sums up both Talmud and the Zohar and many other Jewish literature. The essence of Judaism, especially mystical Judaism, is discussion, discussion, discussion. Everything must be examined and new and improved interpretations are always possible.

It is said that Kabbalah can only really be studied through group discussion and there's a lot of truth in that. Because it's a structure on which to hang our lives, it is constantly interpreted and updated.

How to View the Tree of Life

All of Kabbalah is based on the Tree of Life diagram. We have already taken a brief look at the three columns but, before we even start working out what the diagram means, we first have to decide how we look at it.

The Tree is the image of the perfect human being. You could say that it is the image of Christ or the image of God. Kabbalistic tradition says that it is the image of Adam Kadmon, the name given to the first primordial being. That is where the phrase "Man is made in God's image" comes from originally.

Several Kabbalistic traditions teach that you look at the Tree as though this perfect human is looking back at you; Christian Kabbalah teaches that we look at the Tree in the way that we would look at an image of Jesus Christ. Others teach that it is like looking in a mirror — you are seeing yourself reflected and perfected.

But the oldest tradition teaches that you are looking at the *back* of the perfected human. This way, you can step forward and *into* the diagram. Effectively you are stepping into your own divine self.

Viewed this way, the Tree explains the Biblical phrase: "You cannot look upon the face of God and live." As we are Source energy we would have to disconnect and see ourselves as separate in order to see God's face. There is a similar phrase in Buddhism: "If you see the Buddha on the road, kill him," meaning that you are Buddha; Buddha is in you so any external representation represents separation.

The tree is made up from the ten Sefirot connected by 22 paths. Each Sefira, path and the connecting triangles or *Triads* represents something about you.

11

The Sefirot

There are ten Sefirot, each one depicting an aspect of our life. You can also look at them as archetypes or characteristics. They also equate to the planets of the Solar System and the Greek/Roman gods.

The Tree demonstrates what's known as the Lightning Flash of Creation (fig 4, opposite) showing divine energy zig-zagging diagonally from the top to bottom. The zig-zag is to show the principles of expansion and contraction or duality. The right hand column of the Tree is the active principle (like switching on the electricity to power a kettle) and the left hand column is the passive principle (turning the kettle off so that it doesn't burn up). The central column represents consciousness as we humans decide how active and how passive to be at any given moment. The right-hand column can be summed up as "Yes!" and the left hand one as "No!" Both are needed for balance, which is achieved in the centre.

Keter (crown) represents our Higher Self; our God-selves; the source of the Tree of Life and All-That-Is.

Hokhmah (inspiration, wisdom) is the first impulse; the first flash of an idea that hasn't yet been defined. *I'd love to lead a workshop!*

Binah (understanding) is the catching of that impulse to clarify and define it. *What kind of workshop? Where, when, how?*

These three Sefirot form what are known as the *Supernal Triad* which represents the three aspects of the Divine. Christians might call this the Trinity. In the times of the First Temple in Judaism it represented God the One, God the masculine impulse and God the feminine impulse (known as the Queen of Heaven).

The Lightning Flash then crosses over the dark non-Sefira called *Da'at* to get to *Hesed* on the right hand column.

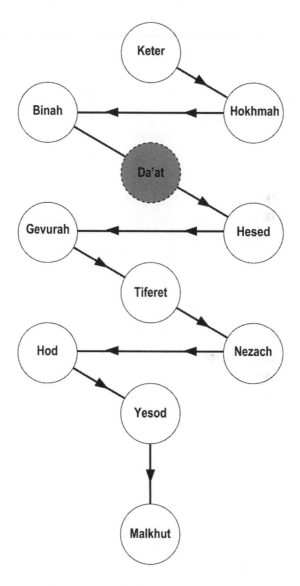

There is no pathway here because it represents both a leap of faith and an act of will. This is the place of the long dark night of the soul and the link point between heaven and the psyche.

Remember how many times you have had a great idea in the middle of the night and then, in the morning either forgotten it or thought *Oops...no that won't work!*

Da'at means knowledge as in intuition and it is also the link between your human self (Tiferet) and your divine self (Keter). I call it the "cat-flap" because it is a window between worlds. It is also the place where anything not strong enough to live (whether physical, spiritual or psychological) falls away. It is also our pathway to a higher consciousness.

On the other side of Da'at is Hesed (loving-kindness or mercy). This is also the place of boundless enthusiasm and, like all the other Sefirot it needs to be tempered by its opposite Sefira so as not to over-balance. If your idea of a workshop gets here it could be summarized by *Yes! This will be wonderful! It will help so many people. It will be such a wonderful thing to do!* (Hesed is definitely the place of exclamation marks).

From there the Lightning Flash crosses back to **Gevurah** (discipline, judgment, discernment) for honing. *Do you know enough? Would people really want this? Is it feasible? Is it truly useful?*

Next is **Tiferet**: your true self. This is the caption of the ship of the psyche; the place where you are conscious and uniquely you; able to choose unity or separation from the Divine. Tiferet means beauty and truth. At Tiferet you are centered, balanced and in touch with the worlds above and below. *Yes. This is right for me. I am the power in my world and I choose to go ahead with this workshop.*

Next step is **Nezach** (initiation of action, attraction, sexuality) a place of impulse and gut feeling, making yourself attractive and going out to meet people, acting before you think and sometimes pushing too hard. *The workshop will look like this and this. The flyers are going out. They will be this colour and this shape. I will send out more and more and contact everyone I know.*

Hod (thought, intellect, reverberation) is the partner of Nezach — the thought processes that balance action. Hod will monitor life's processes and, if out of balance with Nezach will over-think everything. *Is it properly planned? What order shall I do things? Are the flyers working? How many are coming? Is it enough? Should I re-think anything?*

Back on the central column of the Tree we now come to **Yesod** (foundation), the place of the ego; the persona — the masks that we present to the world. Yesod equates to the reticular activating system of the brain which works on repetition. If it is a new experience it will be dealt with by Tiferet, if it has been repeated enough to be learnt, it is dealt with by Yesod. All our reactions and habits are focused here. Yesod is also the child within. If this is your first workshop it will be concerned: *Does it look all right? Have I done the right thing? Does it look good? Will it succeed?* If you have done many successful workshops it will be confident. *It always works; people like my work; I can do this.*

Finally, we are at the bottom of the Tree at **Malkhut** (Kingdom): the place of manifestation. Malkhut is the body, our physical reality or the location of the workshop. Everything is made real in Malkhut and, if it doesn't reach Malkhut, it is stillborn.

12

The Sefirot and Astrology

Kabbalah is also closely associated with astrology mainly because the wise ones of the past who studied the stars were always astrologers as well as astronomers. They didn't write Sun Sign columns or do any generalized astrology which is one of the main reasons why the subject has become so belittled today. Neither did they do much birth time astrology because most folks didn't know when they had been born. Instead they watched the sky for signs and portents "Let there be lights in the firmament of the heaven to divide the day from the night; and let them be for signs and for seasons," it says in Genesis 1:14. They also practiced Horary Astrology which is the art of casting a chart for the time when a certain question is asked such as "Should I marry this man?" A question could only be answered at certain times and the querant would often ask it when there could be no reply given.

Each of the Sefirot of the Tree of Life represents a planet and the Triads (triangles) of the Tree correspond with the signs of the Zodiac (see fig 5, opposite).

The Sefirot reflect the characteristics and archetypes of the planets and the Greek/Roman gods. However, in ancient days, when no one knew about the planets Neptune, Uranus or Pluto they were given different attributes, as shown below. The dispute over whether Pluto is a planet or not does not matter as the whole of the Kuiper belt has an elliptic orbit which moves both inside and outside the orbit of Neptune so it is still a good representation of Da'at as a window between worlds.

Keter — First Swirlings of Creation/Neptune. Rules Pisces.
Hokhmah — The whole Zodiac/Uranus. Rules Aquarius.

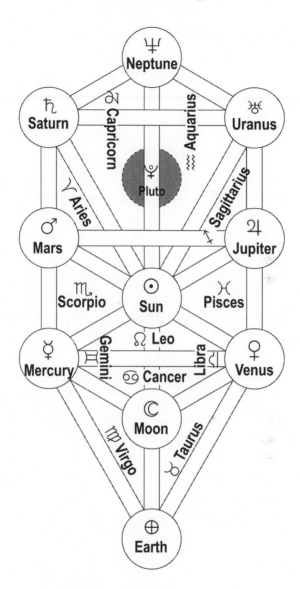

Binah — Saturn. Rules Capricorn.
Da'at— Milky Way/Pluto. Rules Scorpio.
Hesed — Jupiter. Rules Sagittarius.
Gevurah — Mars. Rules Aries.
Tiferet — Sun. Rules Leo.
Nezach — Venus. Rules Taurus and Libra.

33

Hod — Mercury. Rules Gemini and Virgo.
Yesod — Moon. Rules Cancer.
Malkhut — Earth. Rules the Ascendant.

It can be a very useful exercise, if you know your own astro-logical chart, to place it on to the Tree of Life as it is a relatively simple way of understanding what strengths, weaknesses and stresses your chart has. For example, Hod is ruled by the quick-silver of Mercury so it is happy when your Natal Mercury is in Virgo or Gemini and reasonably comfortable with watery signs such as Pisces or Cancer. But Hod in a fire sign such as Leo, Sagittarius or Aries can lead to your appearing arrogant, tactless or sharp in your communications whether you mean to or not. And Hod in Taurus or Capricorn can be slow to react or slow of thinking. None of these is necessarily bad but they are useful to know in case you are planning a career where you need to communicate clearly.

It is important to realise that Astrology is only our default position. We all have free will to make conscious decisions from Tiferet. Astrology is only associated with the watery world of the psyche which is known as Yezirah. But this is the world where we all spend most of our time, in our thoughts and feelings. We think we are physical beings but Kabbalah has always taught that we are a soul with a body temporarily attached and it is our psyches which are the link point between heaven and earth.

13

Jacob's Ladder

The diagram of Jacob's Ladder (fig 6, overleaf) is a cosmic map of how the Holy One designed and created the Universe. It demonstrates the invisible laws of life such as duality and Karma and explains the principles behind planets, angels, humanity, archetypes and good and evil.

Jacob's Ladder is the Tree of Life depicted four times at different levels. The top tree, *Azilut*, is the world of the Divine — the body of the primordial human being called Adam Kadmon. This is the world depicted by the element of fire and it is the origin of all souls. We are all first born from the Soul Triad within Azilut which is known as *The Treasure House of Souls*. Our first journey is down from Azilut through the second world of creation and spirit which is called *Beriah*) where we become human or not and male or female. Then we pass down to *Yezirah*, the World of Forms where we take on our psychological traits to become the individuals that we all are. Finally — for that journey at least — we put on our "coats of skin" and are born into the physical body that inhabits the planet, and the World of Earth. This is known as Assiyah.

The second journey is to make our way back up the Ladder through self-development and spiritual growth. We won't get very far on our first few lives because we have to learn how to live in a physical environment and learn how the tribe/family/ society works and where we fit into it. But once we have got that sorted out, we will start seeking to lift ourselves higher; to experience our soul and spirit and seek reunion with our complete self. This is personified by the Sefira of the Keter of Yezirah, which is also the Tiferet of Beriah and the Malkhut of

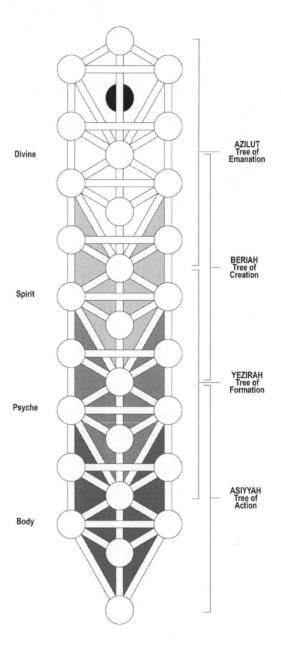

Azilut. Most people know it as the Crown Chakra or the Higher Self. We have direct access to it through the Da'at of Yezirah (which is also the Yesod of Beriah) when we are centered in the

Tiferet of Yezirah (our Solar Plexus Chakra).

The third journey is to teach others and pass on what we have learnt spiritually. In most people, the second and third journeys are taken in parallel in that we experience a little so that we have understood it and then teach it on. It is however very important to do the journeys in that order rather than to teach from what we've heard or read but not actually experienced. If we do that, we can lead others astray.

The fourth journey is to go home, right back up into Azilut as ascended beings. There's much talk in the early 21st century of Ascension as though it is something to be desired above all costs. But most enlightened beings choose to come back to Earth again and again in order to help others up the Ladder. They know also that those who have not incarnated in many centuries could not understand what it is like to live on Earth nowadays. Certainly Universal Principles remain the same but knowledge of the complications of the modern human psyche and experience of physical life are also important to understand the bigger picture and give guidance to incarnate human beings.

Modern Kabbalists studying the New Testament believe that the reason that four gospels were chosen to tell the story of Jesus is because they represent the Four Worlds of Jacob's Ladder — the story of a perfect man who was physically incarnate but also one with all that is divine. It is also a representation of both the first and second temples in the ancient Jewish world.

The Ladder is not the Holy One Itself but the emanation of the Divine Word or, in some cultures, the Divine Song.

Here are some of the attributes of the Four Worlds.

Azilut

Azilut is the world at the top of Jacob's Ladder. It is generally depicted as white, sometimes as gold and represents the element of FIRE. It is the world of emanation; the first aspect of the Divine in existence. The word Azilut means "close to" or "to stand near," because the world of Azilut is not the totality of God but a reflection of a much greater being than we can even begin to conceive of, let alone describe. This is the world of Adam Kadmon, the perfected only-begotten child of God and we are each one cell in that divine being. There is no time, no duality, no male and no female in this world, it is just the pure light flowed into existence by the divine breath and received by the vessels that fill and flow it onwards.

In ancient Kabbalah, this is the world where all is perfect. In Lurianic Kabbalah it is the world where the vessels shattered due to a divine miscalculation. This is a complex concept in a world where all is unity and unchanging.

Interestingly Jacob's Ladder disappeared from the public domain when Lurianic Kabbalah became the main focus of the teaching. This might have been because the new concept was impossible to explain with the Ladder or it may have been due to Luria's own even more complex designs replacing it. Jacob's Ladder only returned to mainstream Kabbalistic teaching in the 1970s — as the wider world began to pick up the concept of the Law of Attraction and Karma.

The Kabbalah Center explains the idea of the broken vessels by saying that the vessels (the Sefirot) that received the light did not wish only to receive but also to give so they rejected the light. After some negotiation, the light was flowed in a lesser way and the teaching of the Center is that it must be flowed on immediately to others. This is a Yeziratic (psychological) interpretation of how people who feel broken themselves in some way (as most of us do) find it easier to give than to receive.

The original teaching was best illustrated by the line in the 23rd Psalm which says "My cup runneth over." If we drink deeply and fully before we then give to others then we are always a receptacle that is full of life, love, abundance and generosity. If we give the second we receive, our cup is always half empty.

Beriah

The next plane of existence, is the world of Beriah, or creation. This is the place where duality begins and where the first limitations are imposed and is the element of AIR. The light that flows down from Azilut becomes slightly more unrefined with every step it takes away from its source.

The two side pillars of Beriah express ultimate creation and ultimate destruction. This implies limited reality, or bringing into being a limited existence. Here there is the first day and night, male and female, up and down.

Another definition of the word Beriah in Hebrew signifies "outside of." This implies a one step of separation from the Infinite Light. That does not mean that the light is less but that it is concealed in some way. No place in the multiverse is actually devoid of divine energy.

Beriah is the world of the Archangels, great cosmic beings who fulfill the will of the Holy One. We tend to create images of the Archangels but there are no images or forms in Beriah so these pictures are a good example of how the idea of something in Beriah is "fleshed out" in our minds at the lower level of Yezirah.

Beriah is pure concept; pure idea; pure thought. It has no emotion.

Yezirah

Yezirah is the world of formation and the element of WATER. Where in Azilut there was the concept of existence and in Beriah the creation of, for example *Dog*, in Yezirah there are the different kinds or forms of dog as in wolf, spaniel, retriever, foxhound. Then in the final world, Assiyah, each physical dog is born and lives.

Concepts are formed into images at this level. This is the liquid world of emotions rather than the airy world of thoughts. We think something and then it is enveloped by how we *feel* about it. As all the worlds are linked together like the fingers of two hands entwined, this is integral to understanding how affirmation and the Law of Attraction work. If we are feeling unhappy, our foggy, grey Yeziratic psyche draws more thoughts that match the feelings down from Beriah. However, if we can access Tiferet, our conscious self (sometimes called "The Watcher") and the part of us that links the three lower worlds we can deliberately choose to think a better, happier thought from Beriah. Doing that will permeate back down into Yezirah and make us feel better.

Yezirah is the world of angels, astrology, Feng Shui and many other tools of development. Because it is watery and flexible we have to take care to remember that these essences are not the final word in our self-development. Knowing your Astrology and the Feng Shui of your house are very useful, because they are the aspects of life which affect us when we are living life on automatic. None of us is wide awake all the time and both our psyches and the planet operate on a matrix to which they default in lieu of conscious thought or action. If you know that you have a Moon/ego that tends towards self-importance or over-analysis then you can watch out for instances of that being reflected back to you in Yezirah and choose to think different (Beriatic) thoughts to clear the situation.

Our souls are the center point of the Yeziratic world. Our individual soul is the essence of being; the focal point of our humanity. While our self is the one-off person alive right now, our soul is the sum total of all our incarnations into which our self will dissolve at death.

Assiyah

Assiyah is the element of EARTH; the final plane or world, which we call physical reality. It is finite not only in space but also in time which means that unlike Yezirah and Beriah, one object cannot be in two places simultaneously and when one thing

40

ceases to be, another thing begins. In Yezirah, a beloved pet has not died, it has just transformed into its eternal soul. It still exists in its essence and it can be remembered and loved. Even more, stories can still be created about it in our minds and its image changed back to when it was young in Assiyah. Many a bereavement has been eased when someone knows how to re-frame the loss of someone or something much loved into a happier Yeziratic memory than the one the "real" world calls the truth.

Time is paramount in Assiyah and it is the most fragile of all the worlds. A physical life can be destroyed in a second and in an increasingly more secular Western World it may be that we grieve more when we experience death because we are not reminded of the soul's continual existence.

Just because a creature on Earth is extinct doesn't mean that it has been erased from the higher worlds. Far from it: the Dodo and many other species are alive and well in Beriah and Yezirah. They may even have incarnated in other physical worlds. Assiyah is the furthest world from the Source but it is also the manifestation of all that is the Source. Without physical reality, God cannot be made manifest in the world; without each human being the Holy One cannot experience the joy of reading, writing, cooking, walking, cuddling, or even eating chocolate. It's important for us to realise that we too are creators; without sentient beings who live in Assiyah and enjoy its beauty and bounty, there is no point to creation.

The Fifth Tree

Many people believe in the Chinese system of five elements rather than four, the fifth element being metal. This fits in with what is known as the Fifth Tree on Jacob's Ladder (fig 7, overleaf). This final tree is the direct link between the Keter of Azilut and the Malkhut of Assiyah and is formed by the ten Sefirot of the central column starting at the bottom with Malkhut

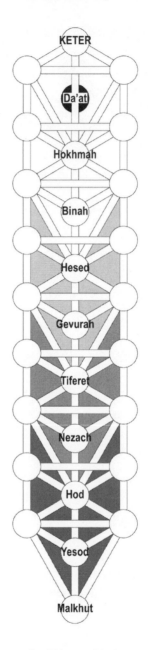

and going all the way up the Tree to Keter.

Christian Kabbalists believe that it was this tree to which John the Baptist was referring when he said to "prepare ye the way of the Lord and make his paths straight." (Matthew 3:3).

The "Our Father" prayer fits on this fifth tree beginning at the Keter of Keters with "Our Father" and flowing down the central column until "Deliver us from evil" at the Malkhut of Malkhuts.

The additional phrases (added later) of "For thine is the Kingdom, the Power and the Glory, for ever and ever" refer to Malkhut, the right hand column of the entire ladder (power). the left hand column (glory) and the central column (eternity). The final "Amen" is a return up the central column to the Keter of Keters.

14

Angels & Archangels

Angels are very popular at the moment with people often saying "I'll ask my angels" rather than "I'll ask God" or "I'll pray."

This is not necessarily new. Kabbalah teaches that each of the ten aspects of the Tree of Life represents a cosmic archetype that was personified by an angel. In other cultures these archetypes were called gods.

Kabbalah teaches that angels are a lower vibrationary essence of archangels which, in turn are part of a great wheel of cosmic beings that serve the Holy One, carry our prayers and messages and supervise the everyday workings of the Universe. The nine ranks of the angels were defined by Pseudo-Dionysius the Areopagite in the sixth century CE as Angels, Archangels, Thrones, Powers, Principalities, Virtues, Dominions, Cherubim and Seraphim.

Back in the time of the First Temple the four great archangelic beings which represented the four elements were known by description rather than title as Wonderful Counselor, the Mighty (one of) God, the Everlasting Father and the Prince of Peace. After the Babylonian exile these four attributes were named Uriel, Gabriel, Raphael and Michael.

Nowadays, the teaching archangels are placed in Beriah, the spiritual world of Jacob's Ladder with their corresponding angels in Yezirah, the psychological and soul world (fig 8, opposite). We humans usually communicate with the angelic level rather than with the archangel itself because the archangels' vibrational level is much stronger and more vibrant than we can comprehend and they are, energetically, the size of a star.

By far the most popular archangel is Michael who is placed at

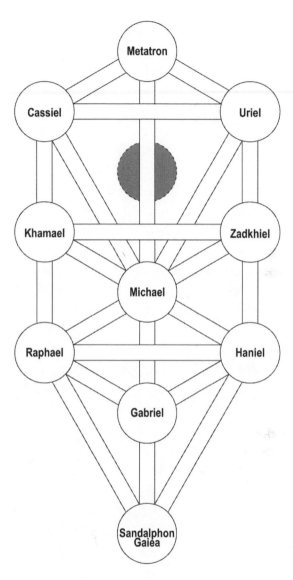

the Malkhut of Azilut, the Tiferet of Beriah and the Keter of Yezirah. Michael therefore has the energetic field of our own Higher Self (Yezirah) the Captain of the Host (Beriah) and Christ (Azilut). He is also the highest energy we can conceive of and frequently invoked for matters involving Khamael (protection) and Zadkiel (prosperity) because those presences are outside Yezirah, the world of Form, and so powerful that they are challenging to our consciousness. The petitions are passed through Michael to the appropriate Archangels and from them to the Holy One.

The angelic correspondences to the Sefirot are:

Keter. This Sefira is primarily associated with *Metatron*, the only known being who is both human and angel. He was once Enoch, the first ascended man who became one with the Divine. Metatron is the access point between God and the rest of creation and the great High Priest. Some people mistakenly refer to Metatron as their guardian or guide but he is the ultimate guide for *all* humanity not individuals. This Sefira is also associated with *Asariel* who rules Neptune and co-rules Thursdays with Zadkiel (Hesed). Asariel represents intuition, imagination and mysticism as well as deception. He represents the gods Neptune or Poseidon. Many people fool themselves that they are being inspired or channeled through when they are not truly in touch with any higher essence. This is one of the negative aspects of the lower Sefira of Hod.

Hokhmah. *Uriel*, Lord of Uranus, who guards the gates of Eden with a flaming sword. Uriel rules lightning, mental health and the nervous system, freedom, revolution, independence, new ideas and divorce. He is associated with Saturday, together with Cassiel and is the Angel of the North. Uranus was the ancient god of the sky and married to Gaeia, goddess of the Earth.

Binah. *Cassiel*, Lord of Karma and the planet Saturn. Cassiel rules bones, old age, solitude, restriction, discipline and strictness, but also acceptance, wisdom and humility. He co-rules Saturday and is the patron of teachers, archeologists and dentists. He represents the gods Cronos and Saturn, who also stand for time and age.

Da'at. *Azrael*, the Lord of Pluto, co-rules Tuesday with Khamael (Gevurah). He is responsible for the passage of deep wisdom and knowledge between the higher and lower worlds and watches over the dangerous influences of Pluto, such as terrorism and fanaticism. The gods Pluto, Hades, Osiris and Anubis are all connected to Azrael, and he is said to be the one who killed all the first-born sons of the Egyptians during the ten plagues.

Hesed: *Zadkiel* also known as *Sachiel* rules Jupiter, co-rules Thursday and portrays justice, generosity, prosperity, finances and freedom from debt. He is the patron of all lawyers, judges, fishermen and mariners. Zadkiel also represents secular pleasures, such as gambling and horse-racing. He is connected with the ancient gods Zeus and Jupiter, the king and father of the other gods. This is because on the extended Tree (the Fifth Tree) Hesed is at the highest point of Yezirah; the place of both Christ and Archangel Michael.

Gevurah: *Khamael* also known as *Samael* is often greatly feared for he is the angel of pure destruction. Khamael rules Mars and co-rules Tuesday. Mars was originally god of agriculture (think weeding, compost and ploughing — "destructive" acts that need to happen for food to be fertilized and grow) and became god of war when we invented fences and began to defend them. He also stands for courage, passion and strength of mind. He is the patron of firemen, sportsmen, surgeons and all people in the military forces. Khamael helps us to find the bravery and strength we need to face obstacles or enemies. His secondary name of Samael has often been inaccurately associated with Satan and his works thought of as evil. As he stands at the place of heavenly destruction, he will break down anything which needs to be destroyed — but nothing which does not. He is a powerful protector and teacher and surprisingly gentle at times. If we ask him to defend us from an enemy, he will often give that enemy a wonderful new job to move them away from us. Khamael can see that there is always responsibility on both sides when there is enmity between people.

Tiferet: *Michael* the Angel of the South, rules the Sun and Sunday and is the patron of all priests and spiritual workers. He rules marriage and the golden wedding ring and legitimate ambition. He also protects from pride, selfishness and egoism. Michael is the sun god — Helios, Apollo, Ra — and the representative of all managing directors and other leaders. He is probably the best-known archangel, the Captain of the Host, leader of the last stand between good and evil, the protector of mankind, and the perfect reflection of divine light. His name means "Who is like unto God?" The question mark is important as it tells us that *no one* is the equivalent of the Holy One.

Nezach: *Haniel*, the Lord of Venus rules Friday. Haniel is one of two archangels (Gabriel is the other) who is sometimes depicted as feminine. Haniel represents grace, beauty, harmony, music, attraction, love and affection. Haniel is also the angel of the devas and fairies and, at that level, sex. Misused, her energy makes a god of glamour; correctly petitioned, she can bring love, reconcile lovers and support family links. The goddesses associated with her are Venus and Aphrodite.

Hod: *Raphael*, the Angel of the East, rules Mercury and Wednesday and is associated with the god of the same name also known as Hermes and Thoth. Raphael is the primary archangel of healing because he rules thought, communication, travel and speed. Most of our sicknesses are caused by dis-eased thought or over-doing things and Raphael helps us to slow down and rest. He is also patron of language, translation, writing, communication, the Internet and the News. The later often represent the Mercurial aspect of "the trickster" where we can be made to believe things which are not necessarily true... Hod is also the Sefira of psychic awareness as opposed to spiritual awareness.

Yesod: *Gabriel,* the Angel of the West, the only angel to be mentioned by name in the Koran, is best known for telling the Virgin Mary that she would be the mother of Jesus. Gabriel is responsible for the Moon and Monday. Where Raphael represents communication between humans, Gabriel is the messenger from God to humanity. She is also patron of the home, pets, lilies, feelings in general and intuition. Gabriel's equivalents in mythology include Isis, Astarte, Artemis and Diana. She is the patron of doctors, nurses, midwives, nannies and teachers.

Malkhut. *Sandalphon* or *Gaeia.* Sandalphon is the physical rendition of Metatron and said to be the guardian of all the prayers sent up to the Holy One. We know this level better as Gaeia, goddess of the Earth who represents the ancient goddess Ceres.

15

Exercises and Rituals

Many Kabbalists get lost in theory but Kabbalah is meant to be experienced through action as well as contemplation. Here are some simple exercises and rituals that you can use both to experience the Tree of Life and its balancing effect in your life.

Making The Tree of Life With Your Body
In this exercise use your own physical body to rise up the Tree and then down again, experiencing each Sefira through your physical senses.

Raising yourself up the Tree is a wonderful prayer for opening up and moving down it an effective way of closing down energy after a workshop or a busy day.

> **Malkhut.** Stand with your legs slightly apart and lean down to touch your toes or as near as you can to signify grounding yourself. Say *Malkhut, the Kingdom, the Body.*
> **Yesod.** Stand upright and place your hands on your lower stomach just on the uterus for a woman and above the sex organs for a man. Say *Yesod, the Foundation, the Ego.*
> **Hod.** Lean slightly on to your left foot. This is the first time you will be out of balance away from the central column. See how it makes you feel. Say *Hod, The Way, Reverberation.*
> **Nezach.** Lean slightly on to your right foot. See how that side of the Tree makes you feel. Say *Nezach, The Life, Action.*
> **Tiferet.** Stand upright with your hands on your Solar Plexus. Seek for balance and contemplate the eternal Now. Say *Tiferet, Beauty, Truth.*
> **Gevurah.** Stand upright with your left arm extended at

shoulder height and palm down. Say *Gevurah. Discipline, Discernment, Judgment.*

Hesed. Stand upright, with your right arm extended at shoulder height and palm down. Say *Hesed. Loving Kindness. Mercy.*

Da'at. Stand upright. Look up and turn the palms of both your hands upwards to receive from the higher worlds. Say *Da'at. Knowledge. Gnosis.*

Binah. Stand upright and hold your left arm diagonally up to the left. Say *Binah. Understanding, Boundaries.*

Hokhmah. Stand upright and hold your left arm diagonally up to the right. Say *Hokhmah. Inspiration, Wisdom.*

Keter. Stand upright with both hands in the prayer position above your head. Say *Keter. The Crown. My Higher Self.*

Then draw down the energy of the Crown Chakra to your heart with your hands still in the prayer position. Say *From Thee comes all Grace.*

If you want to close yourself down after a ritual or workshop, or even at the end of a busy day, reverse the movements above until you end up leaning down to touch the floor.

Drawing Your Own Tree Of Life.

Drawing the Tree of Life freehand is a very powerful exercise for seeing how in balance or out of balance we are at this moment.

All you have to do is copy a diagram of the Tree of Life with a pen or pencil. Which Sefirot are large or small and which lines you draw incorrectly or miss out are indications of levels of comfort or discomfort in your psyche and your body. Don't over-think this; it's only about how you are *now* so if you are feeling tired or have just received a big bill, you're not going to draw a perfect Tree. However, it is true to say that if you repeatedly draw the same imbalances for weeks on end, there is an inner stress that is trying to catch your attention.

If any of the Sefirot are particularly larger or smaller than the others, then it is an indication that you are particularly strong or weak in that area. It is the same with the Triads (the triangular areas between the Sefirot). Large circles on the right of the Tree may mean that you do too much. A large Hesed implies that you over-give to others instead of taking care of yourself.

A Tree that is cramped at the top means that you are not finding enough time for your spiritual life or to receive inspiration. A Tree that is cramped at the bottom indicates that you are not giving enough attention to your physical body and its needs, whether that's better food or more exercise.

If the circles of the Sefirot are not closed and if any of the paths you have drawn over-run and break into the Sefirot, you may have a weakness in your psychological boundaries in that area. For example, if the paths from Nezach and Hesed break into Tiferet, you are over-active to the point of not listening to your own truth.

If any of the paths narrow or broken, the Sefirot which are linked by them may have trouble communicating with each other. For example, if there's an unclear path between Hod and Gevurah you may find it hard to make a decision based on the information you have gathered and you may be all theory and no discernment.

If any of the paths are very wide, you may be over-focusing on those two Sefirot. For example, if the path between Nezach and Yesod is very wide you may be obsessed with your own sexuality or public image.

If you forget to fill in any of the paths, then it is an indication that this part of your psyche is not being used, or is being under-used. For example, if you forget the path between Gevurah and Hesed, you have not been focusing on your soul's development.

If your left-hand Sefirot are larger than your right-hand Sefirot, you have a tendency to be over-critical, very concerned with information rather than action or over-judgmental.

If your right-hand Sefirot are larger than your left-hand Sefirot, you are likely to be either over-active, an over-giver, overly pushy or to act before you think.

Oddly enough just drawing out The Tree precisely, using a ruler and either a compass or coins to draw around will help to restore balance. It helps you to focus on who you want to be and that is an effective start for all levels of healing.

Create a Kabbalistic healing room or working space.
Most sacred places have an altar or a place of focus in the East or, in the case of Islam facing Mecca. However, if the Eastern side of the room is not suitable you can create a "spiritual East" with Kabbalistic placement of signs and symbols.

First, cleanse the space either with a smudge stick or incense, by sounding a Tibetan Singing Bowl or drumming or by lighting a white candle. You can do all four if you like! Then place images of the four archangels of the first Temple, who represent the four compass points of the world and their winds. Where you intend the altar or focus point to be will place your image of Raphael to make it your "spiritual East."

Raphael in the East.
Gabriel in the West.
Uriel in the North.
Michael in the South.

It is unlikely that you will be able to put objects representing all the Sefirot in their correct place in a working room but you will get a good enough effect by placing something representing the physical world, either a rock or a crystal, a plant or an image of a mountain in the West for Malkhut.

On the left wall in the North-West position place books or a computer; something representing the intellect and learning. On the opposite, North-West side place something representing

53

dance, sexuality, action or pleasure — perhaps a statue or a picture.

If you can, place a table with flowers or a candle in the middle of the room representing Tiferet. On the left-hand wall an image of a soldier, a Samurai or perhaps gardening implements would fit Gevurah and to the right an image of genuine love or abundance would be perfect for Hesed.

In the North-East and North-West positions you can place representations of wise people or sources of spiritual inspiration and, on the altar itself, whatever represents the sacred to you.

If you have prayers or affirmations, place a copy on the altar to be blessed and whenever you have a new project put something that represents it on that altar too in order to make the work sacred to you and to the Holy One.

Chanting the Holy Name.

The Holy One has ten names (fig 9, opposite); the three most important being the ones that given to Moses at the Burning Bush. These are *Eheyeh Asher Eheyeh*, *Yahveh* and *Elohim* (Exodus 3:14-15) and are the names attributed to the Supernal Triad of Keter, Hokhmah and Binah.

The name Yahweh (Jehovah) is usually the one referred to as "The Great Name" of God. At Hokhmah, its most literal translation is "The Wisdom of God" but the most accepted meaning of the name is "He Brings Into Existence Whatever Exists." Many people think that Jehovah means a fierce and harsh god but that aspect of Divinity is *Yah*, meaning the Judgment of God which is placed at the Gevurah of Azilut (see fig opposite).

Yahweh is spelt, in Roman letters, as YHVH. There are no vowels to the name as Biblical Hebrew was not written in vowels. To pronounce the consonants, Yod-Hey-Vav-Hey, is still a profound experience.

To chant the letters (you can make up your own melody) is to invoke the wisdom of the Divine.

You can chant the Divine Name at any time or in any place,

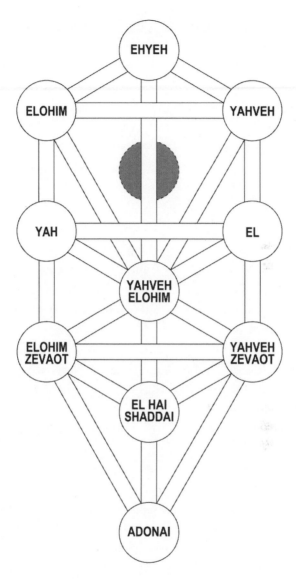

especially to help balance you if you are distressed. But the most fulfilling way to do it is sitting peacefully in a quiet room, having lit two white candles, to represent the side pillars of the Tree of Life. If you can chant it with a friend, the power is greater. It can be sung either in unison or as a round; both are filled with beauty and Grace.

It is said that the highest of the ranks of Archangels continually chant the ten names of God. If you go deep within yourself and listen at a frequency that is outside our normal hearing, you may be blessed enough to hear this great chorus of song that is expressed in indescribable glory without form.

A Kabbalistic Contemplative Meditation.

You may wish to record this meditation so that you can listen to it.

Sit deep in your chair and allow yourself to relax. Feel the weight of your body, the physical world of Assiyah. Feel the liquids within you; the watery world of Yezirah, the blood in your veins; the lymphatic liquids, the saliva in your mouth. Breathe deeply and experience the Beriatic world of air – the oxygen being filtered through your lungs and being carried around your body to fill it with life.

Feel the warmth of your body and sense the radiance of Azilut – the auric fields around you, dancing with light.

Imagine that it is summer. See yourself standing in a country road, outside a closed wicket gate which leads into a private orchard. Beyond it, there is a walled vegetable garden and, beyond that, there is a great bower of climbing plants.

Before you enter, turn and look behind you at the road you took to this place. What does it look like? Is it a country lane, or a wide thoroughfare? Is it a place you are glad to be leaving or a place of contentment?

Lift the latch on the gate and walk into the orchard. What kind of trees are here? Are they flowering or fruiting? What kind of condition are they in? Are they blighted or healthy? Do you see ivy or mistletoe? What is the scent of the orchard like? Is there any sound – birdsong, wind rustling leaves; the soft thump of a falling apple?

Take a moment, as you stand among the trees to consider your five senses. Your ability to see; to hear, to touch, to taste, to identify scents and smells. Realise how subtly important these are to you and spend a moment in the orchard appreciating them. Maybe there is a fruit you can touch, smell, pick, and eat?

Now walk forward to the vegetable garden. Is this walled or open? Is it well-kept or weedy? What kind of vegetables are growing – and what stage are they at? Are they healthy? Is there anything surprising there?

You see a fork and a hoe leaning against a nearby tree. Are you tempted to use them? Or do you just want to wander and look? Is there anything that particularly needs doing here?

Become aware of how delicate and fragile the flowers and fruit around you really are. One careless movement or footstep and you could destroy them. See also, the caterpillars and the greenfly; the ants and the ladybirds, all following their own set lives, eating the leaves, the vegetables and fruit.

Reflect on the fruits of your own life and how many projects and ideas were nibbled away before they could grow to fruition; how many good ideas were smothered by weeds; how much beauty was blighted by the blemish of disbelief in the possibility of fruition. Was it your disbelief or other people's?

Now come to the edge of the vegetable garden to a great over-grown bower of climbing plants. At your feet there are lilies of the valley, pale lobelia and daisies. It looks like the entrance to a secret garden and you want to find your way through – but where is the door?

To your left there is a seat in an archway; it looks comfortable and you could sit there and rest. To your right, there is a gap between the wall and the bower. You slip through it and find yourself walking in a maze with high hedges on either side. You look, and look for a door through to the garden but there is no sign. You walk and walk and walk – and eventually, you find yourself right back at the place you started.

There is the seat and you sit down, feeling tired and frustrated. The sun is warm and you can hear birdsong. The vegetable garden and the orchard look pretty and abundant. Perhaps this is enough for today. Is there really any need to go any further?

Suddenly, you realise that the birdsong is coming from inside the garden, not outside. You feel revitalized, wanting, wanting to go further. You stand up, close your eyes and slip your hand through the dangling greenery right in front of you. And find the handle of a door. You turn it; it opens and you slip through the dangling greenery inside the secret garden.

It is filled with colour – sharp yellow, black and white combinations, soft browns and greens, dusky hues; everywhere you look there are clever designs of flowers; combinations which look like complicated arrangements. The scents in the air are fleeting, sharp, even spiky. Where there is grass it is rich with clover. It is a quicksilver garden with new things to look at every moment. The air is buzzing with life, darting bees and hover-flies. It's an exciting place where no sooner have the petals of one flower fallen than another bloom appears.

You feel stimulated and observant; bright and smart. An idea comes to you – a clever thought – can you catch it? - and then, as the rustle of a bird in a bed of larkspur distracts you, it is gone. Are you comfortable or uncomfortable in this Mercurial garden?

You walk on, until a heavy scent of warm, dusky roses draws you into a garden of exotic wonder of blues and pinks and delicate cream – waxy, elegant, magnificent orchids are everywhere. And there's an image of Aphrodite herself - a sensual statue carved from warm-pink stone wreathed in falling blossom. Dahlias, carnations, delphiniums, pink wild sweet peas, honeysuckle and bluebells - an abundance of everything bright, beautiful and scented.

You stretch, feeling the powerful deep sexuality and life-force within you, inhaling the deep primeval scent of fulfillment. It would be easy to stop here and luxuriate and dream...or would it? How does this Venusian garden feel to you – tempting or overpowering?

But you walk on, finding steps in the path before you, lifting you up so that you can see clearly the way before you – and behind you. The light grows brighter and alongside the steps the flowers are golden orange – marigolds, Chinese lanterns and as you walk on, great, vibrant sunflowers. This is the garden of the Sun. At the top of the steps is a small summer house and here, the sound of bird song rises in crescendo.

Someone is in the summer house, waiting for you. It is the person who takes care of this garden – your inner teacher. You may be able to see them clearly or only sense their presence. They invite you to come into the summer house and sit with them for a while, reflecting on what you have seen and experienced so far on your journey.

They ask you a particular question. How does it make you feel? Can you answer it? They give you a drink of some kind – it tastes of sunlight and it strengthens you as if you had been wrapped in a protective robe of golden light.

Your teacher gives you a staff to carry on the rest of your journey and indicates that it is time to move on. You will see each other again soon.

You get up – and find that your clothing is different. What are you wearing? Are you even the same sex as you were when you set out on your journey? You are considering the changes deeply as you walk on and it is a moment or two before you notice the change in your surroundings.

The garden has become much sparser. Now it is more of a wood filled with holly and yew trees. Dark greens and bright reds abound and the air is noticeably cooler. The grasses, plants and trees have spiky edges to them and you need to make your way with care.

Under your feet you aware of dead leaves crunching and breaking down, each one rotting and dissolving until it becomes new and fertile soil.

Even so, there is a cleanliness of air here that is very refreshing – almost like the scent of the sea but brighter and sharper. You lose concentration for a moment and then jump as a trailing vine with serrated edge cuts your left hand. A small drop of blood forms and falls to the ground. You watch in amazement as a scarlet flower grows and blooms exactly where it fell.

This is a deeply powerful place. The place of Mars, the warrior; the place of life or death. You may not feel comfortable here but you may feel powerful and strong – or you may want to move on swiftly. Whichever, you find yourself walking differently; more alert, assessing each step and staying watchful.

As you walk on, the dark green leaves of the trees broaden and become more succulent. You recognise laurels and then the first tight buds of Rhododendron. Within a few more steps they have flowered in great swathes of purples and pinks. Now you are walking in a great, wood of tall trees with slanting, hot sunlight breaking through. Around you are hydrangeas, Morning Glory, great, deep-coloured purple lilacs and anemone. It's a palace of grand beauty, the great trees meeting high, high overhead in sacred arches of colour. The expansive garden of Jupiter, a place to dance for joy.

You wander and look and listen to the sounds of exotic birds high overhead and then, after a while you realise that this place never seems to end. Is there any way out? Is this it? If so, it's certainly beautiful but somehow it would be so easy to be trapped in this lazy magnificent abundance, never moving on. You know there is something beyond and you begin, actively to seek it.

At last, when you are beginning to feel overwhelmed, even threatened, by all the majesty of your surroundings, you see the lake. It is dark, deep and still and surrounded by bulrushes. Moored nearby is a small boat and you know that the only way onwards, is across that lake.

Carefully, you climb into the boat and cast off. To your surprise, the boat begins to move of its own accord and all you have to do is sit there. It glides out onto the open water and through a patch of water lilies, all in flower with dragon-flies darting across them. You catch a glimpse of fish below – great carp moving slowly in the deep and tiny fry darting here and there.

It appears to be growing dark; you look up and see great rain clouds overhead threatening. A flash of lighting lights the sky, thunder rolls and the heavens open. You are soaked. Even worse, the little boat is beginning to fill with water. How do you feel? After all, this was meant to be a pleasant stroll through a pretty garden, not a dangerous expedition.

A heavy cloud sinks over the boat; the rain has stopped but now you are in fog. It's cold and it's miserable and you want to go home.

Gradually, the fog lightens and you can see sunlight ahead. Even better, the water is becoming shallow and you can see a shore ahead.

It's moorland. A great open space of tough grasses, bare rocks and bracken. You clamber out of the boat and feel sunlight and a brisk warm wind dry your soaking clothes and bring strength to your bones. There's nothing much to see here other than the horizon and some hardy shrubs but it's a solid and reliable landscape; firm beneath the feet. You walk for a while, thinking over your journey and enjoying the feeling of the open air. Ahead of you is a stone circle; grey and solid. Unlike most of the henges you have seen, it is complete.

This is the place of Saturn; boundaries, age and experience. Is it too bleak and strong for you or is this comforting?

You walk inside the circle and see the world within expanding, rising up before you in the form of a hill there is a white temple on it.

You hurry upwards and, as you come closer to the temple, the ground softens and you are aware of the scent of lilies. Excitement – darting, excitement fills you. There they are, clustering around the stones, great white, magnificent waxy flowers rising from a bed of tiny periwinkles, blue as the sky above.

You slip between the stones and follow a path of violets to the temple door, which is surrounded by silvery clematis. Anything could happen around this temple – Uranus rules here. Even the landscape shivers and shimmers as if reality could change any minute. You could change your mind in a second and be back exactly where you started.

You step into the temple. Inside it is a place of soft, silvery blue light on white stone. There is an altar with a closed book on it before you and, above you a dome of gold. This is a place of strength, beauty and peace.

You stand before the altar and look down at the book. It has your true name on the cover. Carefully, you open it and read what is written on the page you have chosen. It may be words; or a picture, or just an impression. Whatever it is it swirls and moves in strands of mist and light. Neptunian, vague, but deep and strong.

One thing you do know; this is the place where questions are answered. And you know what you truly want to ask. You close your eyes and form the question in your mind.

Light forms around you, and celestial voices whisper songs of glory and hope in your ears. You find yourself lifted, floating upwards, held by a thousand angelic thoughts. Up, up, up. It is cool and bright and you open your eyes to see the whole blue universe filled with stars. Up, up, up and then there is only light. Light that should be blinding but is not. Light that is strength, love, understanding and wisdom. You are before the throne of the Divine.

You hear the Voice:

Be still and know that I am God.
Ask your question.
Be still and know that I am God.
Hear the answer.
Be still and know that I am God.

The light lessens, the angelic touch draws you down into the great cosmic sky, through the universes and back down, down, down into the little temple hidden in the heart of the standing stones.

You are alone before the altar and, lying on the book, before you is a gift. Something you have always wanted – represented in a symbol that you can take with you. Pick it up and place it in your heart.

You hear a sound behind you and turn. Your teacher is standing there and you go to them. Together you walk outside the temple and find a seat within the standing stones where you can talk and be, and think.

Here is someone who understands your very soul. Someone who can offer you all the love you believed you did not have. Someone who believes in you in a way no one has ever believed in you before.

Talk and listen. Talk and listen. Listen.

It is time to go. The thought of the long journey home is overwhelming, but your teacher laughs. There is a short cut, and they will show you the way.

You follow as the teacher sets off through the great stones and, straight before you, you see a path. It rises into the air like a bridge over the great plain and, as you walk it, you find yourself crossing above the lake, with the great forest to your left and the dark, sharp woods to your right.

Before you know it you are back at the summerhouse surrounded by golden flowers and butterflies, feeling the heat and strength of the sun shining on your shoulders, filling you with warmth and life. You teacher bids you farewell and tells you that you can return any time you like. They will always be waiting for you.

You are directed to follow another path which takes you straight down to the great bower of pink and white rambling roses, ivy, convolvulus all mixed in together and the door, through to the vegetable garden and the orchard.

You slip through the door and watch as the great swathe of branches and flowers swing back across it to hide it again behind you. Then you look across the vegetable garden. Has anything changed?

Walk on to the orchard, has anything here changed?

And now, there is the wicket gate back to the everyday world. You open it, walk through and close it behind you.

It is time to come back to your body. Feel the warmth within you and around you. Feel the warmth of your body and sense the radiance of Azilut – the auric fields of light around you.

Breathe deeply and experience the Beriatic world of air – the oxygen being filtered through your lungs and being carried around your body to fill it with life.

Feel the liquids within you; the watery world of Yezirah, the blood in your veins; the lymphatic liquids, the saliva in your mouth.

Feel the weight of your body, the physical world of Assiyah. Now stretch and press your feet down onto the floor to reconnect to the world and when you are ready come back into your physical world.

Simple Celebration Ritual

This is based on the Jewish Friday evening ritual called *The Inauguration of the Sabbath* and represents the drawing down of Shekhinah, *The Daughter of the Voice*, a representation of the Malkhut of Azilut and often referred to as the Presence of God or the feminine aspect of the Divine. This is the aspect of God which gives birth to souls into the physical world and receives them back at the time of death.

It is ideal to do this ceremony in the evening at dusk, on the day before a day of rest.

Traditionally, a woman takes the part of Shekhinah and a man performs the rest of the ceremony, taking the Divine essence that she has transmitted from Azilut, through Beriah and down through the Yezirah to Assiyah.

In a home where there is a same-sex partnership or two friends living together, one should voluntarily take the part of the sacred feminine and the other the sacred masculine. However, it is perfectly permissible to do it on your own if you live alone.

You will need:

- Two candles,
- Wine or grape juice.
- Either one glass to share or enough glasses for all present.
- A bowl of water, a jug and a clean towel.
- Two bread rolls covered with a clean cloth. Salt.

The first part of the service represents Azilut.

The woman/feminine says a short prayer of blessing or invocation. These are the traditional Jewish words:

"Lord of the Universe, I am about to perform the sacred duty of kindling the lights in honor of the Sabbath. Even as it is written: 'And Thou shalt call the Sabbath a delight and the holy day of the Lord honorable.'

"And may the effect of my fulfilling this commandment be that the stream of abundant life and heavenly blessing flow in upon me and mine. That Thou be gracious unto us and cause thy presence to dwell among us.

"Father of mercy, O continue thy loving kindness unto me and unto my dear ones. Make me worthy to walk in the way of the righteous before thee, loyal to thy law and clinging to good deeds. Keep Thou far from us all manner of shame, grief and care and grant that peace, light and joy ever abide in our home. For with thee is the fountain of life; in thy light do we see light. Amen."

The woman/feminine then lights the candles and makes a circular movement with both hands around them from the outside, round the back and towards herself. On the third movement, having brought the light down through the three lower worlds, she puts her hands over her face to draw the Divine into her.

She then pours the wine, linking the worlds of Azilut and Beriah.

The man/male then says an appropriate blessing. Here is a shortened version of the Jewish prayer:

"Blessed art thou O Lord our God, King of the Universe, who created the fruit of the vine.

"Blessed at thou O Lord our God, King of the Universe, who hast sanctified us by thy commandments and hast taken pleasure in us, and in love and favor has given us thy holy Sabbath as an inheritance. Blessed art thou O Lord who makes the Sabbath holy."

All those taking part inhale the scent of the wine and then drink, experiencing the Worlds of Beriah and Yezirah.

Next each person present washes their hands. Traditionally one pours water from a jug over the others hands and into a bowl below. This represents the watery world of Yezirah.

The normal blessing here is:

"Blessed art thou O Lord our God who hast sanctified us by thy commandments and commanded us concerning the washing of hands. Yezirah."

Finally, salt the bread and break it to distribute around all those present. The traditional prayer is:

"Blessed art thou O Lord our God who brings forth bread from the earth."

This represents the physical world of Assiyah and the two bread rolls are emblems of the fact that the next day is a day of rest where food is already provided.

Conclusion

It is hard to understand the richness of Kabbalah from a book but hopefully these pages will have shown you whether or not you wish to continue to study or use this particular tool for your self-development or spiritual growth.

People often ask "What use is Kabbalah?" The answer is that understanding the Tree of Life will help you to appreciate the conscious and subconscious attributes of your psyche and how they relate to the great archetypes of the Universe and to the Holy One Itself.

Just contemplating the difference between Yesod (ego and persona) and Tiferet (the true self) will help you to realise just how much of your life is lived on automatic and how much is lived consciously. It is said that 95% or more of our thoughts are the thoughts that we thought yesterday — that is repetitive and therefore Yesodic. Tiferet is the place of the new where we think new thoughts, re-pent, re-member, re-consider. The Greek word for "repentance" is *metanoia* which means to think anew.

A good example of living from Tiferet is to observe your thoughts and feelings dispassionately. To say "This is me thinking this" will detach you slightly from the feeling of the thought itself and help you to see yourself and your thoughts in a new light. Even doing this for five minutes a day can have a profound effect on the quality of life and perception.

Both the popular Sedona Method and the work of Byron Katie are Kabbalistic in approach in that they encourage us to look at old long-thought and felt issues and to reinterpret them in order to see them in a new light.

If Kabbalah interests you and you want to know more there is a list of recommended reading after the Bibliography. However, your best step is to find a Kabbalistic study group. There are multitudes of online groups (many associated with the Kabbalah

Center which may not be your particular cup of tea). You can also start your own group by getting together with friends and discussing a chapter of a particular book. There is an old saying that when the pupil is ready, the teacher will appear.

Go well.

Bibliography

Way of Kabbalah, Z'ev ben Shimon Halevi. Kabbalah Society.

A Kabbalistic Universe. Z'ev ben Shimon Halevi. Kabbalah Society.

Adam and the Kabbalistic Trees. Z'ev ben Shimon Halevi. Kabbalah Society.

The Hidden Tradition of The Kingdom of God, Margaret Barker. SPCK.

Sacred Magic of the Angels. David Goddard. Weiser.

Gnosis of the Cosmic Christ: A Gnostic Christian Kabbalah. Tau Malachi. Llewellyn.

The Illustrated History of Kabbalah. Maggy Whitehouse. Lorenz.

Recommended Further Reading

Selected Poems of Solomon Ibn Gabirol. Princeton University Press.

The Complete Guide to the Kabbalah: How to Apply the Ancient Mysteries of the Kabbalah to Your Everyday Life. Will Parfitt. Rider & Co.

World of Kabbalah. Z'ev ben Shimon Halevi. Kabbalah Society.

Kabbalah: School of the Soul. Z'ev ben Shimon Halevi. Kabbalah Society.

Temple Themes in Christian Worship Margaret Barker. T & T Clark.

Kabbalistic Tradition: An Anthology of Jewish Mysticism. Alan Unterman. Penguin Classics.

The Tree of Sapphires, David Goddard. Weiser.

Total Kabbalah. Maggy Whitehouse. Chronicle.

B O O K S

O is a symbol of the world, of oneness and unity. In different cultures it also means the "eye," symbolizing knowledge and insight. We aim to publish books that are accessible, constructive and that challenge accepted opinion, both that of academia and the "moral majority."

Our books are available in all good English language bookstores worldwide. If you don't see the book on the shelves ask the bookstore to order it for you, quoting the ISBN number and title. Alternatively you can order online (all major online retail sites carry our titles) or contact the distributor in the relevant country, listed on the copyright page.

See our website **www.o-books.net** for a full list of over 500 titles, growing by 100 a year.

And tune in to myspiritradio.com for our book review radio show, hosted by June-Elleni Laine, where you can listen to the authors discussing their books.

MySpiritRadio